ARCHITECTURAL SKETCHING IN MARKERS

Architectural Sketching in Markers

Written by Harold Linton
Illustrated by Roy J. Strickfaden

VNR VAN NOSTRAND REINHOLD
New York

To the Strickfaden family:
Monica, Joni, Matthew,
Lea, Gail, Carol,
Peter, Ann, Tom, Sue,
Joanne Galloway, and Joe Malonis.

Designed by Harold Linton
Illustrated by Roy J. Strickfaden

Full-page illustrations:

Frontispiece—Commercial Building Entrance, Collection of Roy Strickfaden
Page viii—Defining the Concept, Collection of Roy Strickfaden
Page 68—Establishing Form and Space, Collection of Roy Strickfaden
Page 128—Visual References, Collection of Roy Strickfaden

Copyright © 1991 by Harold Linton and Roy J. Strickfaden

Library of Congress Catalog Number 90-12162
ISBN 0-442-31883-9

Printed in the United States of America

Van Nostrand Reinhold
115 Fifth Avenue
New York, New York 10003

Van Nostrand Reinhold International Company Limited
11 New Fetter Lane
London EC4P 4EE, England

Van Nostrand Reinhold
480 La Trobe Street
Melbourne, Victoria 3000, Australia

Nelson Canada
1120 Birchmount Road
Scarborough, Ontario M1K 5G4, Canada

16 15 14 13 12 11 10 9 8 7 6 5 4 3 2 1

Library of Congress Cataloging-in-Publication Data

Linton, Harold.
    Architectural sketching in markers/by Harold Linton and Roy Strickfaden.
        p. cm.
    Includes bibliographical references (p.   ).
    ISBN 0-442-31883-9
    1. Architectural drawing. 2. Dry marker drawing.
I. Strickfaden, Roy J., 1928–   . II. Title.
NA2726.3.L56   1990
720'.28'4—dc20   90-12162
                                                                        CIP

Contents

Foreword

The ability to quickly and skillfully jot down visual notes, capture the essence of a concept, and effectively communicate both complex and basic ideas to others is truly critical to the architectural design process. It requires a confident hand, a clever mind, and the ability for both to work simultaneously. The work of Roy Strickfaden, architect and illustrator, shows that he is able to do just this.

The relationship between an architect's thinking, sketching, and seeing is an essential part of the design and illustration processes. The author leads us into the graphic activities of defining a concept in Part One with a discussion of works created for the purposes of spatial analysis, effective visual viewpoint, and methods of quick and refined sketching. He then gives ample demonstration of exterior and interior subjects, cityscapes, furnishings, landscape, and entourage, with commentary regarding the effective use of markers for the color sketch and refined illustration.

The mastery of his work comes in part from his ability to relate techniques of transparent watercolor painting to graphic methods in marker drawing. He has been inspired by and studied with such fine watercolorists as Ted Kautzky, Robert Wood, Bud Shackleford and Dong Kingman. A colleague, Harvey Ferrero, once remarked. "Watching him work on his drawings is as delightful as viewing the finished product." His ability to present architectural subject matter in forceful, colorful detail has earned him an envied reputation among his colleagues and in the professional world.

RICHARD ROCHON
Advisory Council
American Society of Architectural Perspectivists

Preface

The essence of effective drawing is defining the reaction between light and form. At the heart of this process is the designer's eye searching the subject for its essential qualities of contrast, and the basic means of line, form, and texture to convey the idea without embellishment. The intention of this text is to focus on architectural sketching with marker pens; its reward is an insight gained via exposure and experience that leads to a deeper awareness of visual communication and ultimately to a greater facility to express color, light, form, and space quickly in the design process.

Sketching is a spontaneous and intuitive activity that is also a means to an end—it informs, qualifies, and directly contributes to the formation of a work of design. Interior, architectural, and environmental designers propagate images quickly to represent design concepts. A look at an idea is best realized in a series of brief studies that may be extended at a later date from exploratory sketching to intermediate drawing with added detail and then to highly detailed final renderings and illustrations. Markers are an ideal tool for use during the early stages of the design process: they offer the capability of an immediate response to form, space, and levels of illumination through marker value ranges of warm and cool temperature grays, and to color and texture through an ever-widening palette of hues with the supportive technology of blenders, airbrushes, and color-mixing components.

The works included in this study contain a wide variety of preliminary sketches and provide readers with a perception of individual methods in value analysis and color representation. Many images were produced in series groupings, making it possible to compare and discuss graphic methods toward the particular expression of an environment and the relevant effects of color, light, form, and space. Most important, seeing an extensive body of sketches defuses speculation that a single drawing might be the result of serendipity rather than the intentional summation of the illustrator's ideas about design and how to represent them. The author's intent is to underscore an *economy of means* in the act of drawing and sketching, and to communicate how the essential ingredients of a subject or concept can be distilled and portrayed with deliberate, simple stroke form. Accordingly, the gallery of drawings by the author in Part One and the portfolios by several well-known and emerging architects and illustrators included in Part Four should provide readers with greater insights into the relation between sketch images and methods of design and illustration. It is hoped that architects and designers will use this study as a catalyst for creating original compositions throughout the design process.

The images in Parts One through Three were created by the author, often as demonstrations in the classroom workshop or as conversational drawings directly with the client. They have been selected to demonstrate marker sketching concepts in series. Each series is indicated as such in the text and is often accompanied by related discussion in the figure captions.

Acknowledgment and appreciation is extended to Richard Rochon; Karl Greimel, Dean, College of Architecture and Design at Lawrence Technological University; Gretchen Rudy, research and editorial associate; Elizabeth Govan, graphic associate; Wally Bizon, photographer; David Barton, graphic assistant; Everett Smethurst, Senior Editor, Architecture, and Paul Lukas, Editorial Supervisor, Van Nostrand Reinhold; the portfolio contributors, for their kind contributions; all of the architects who granted Roy Strickfaden permission to reproduce illustrations of their works, and whose names are listed in the Design Credits section in the book.

Part One:
Defining the Concept

The Sketch

It is important to note at the outset that an architectural illustration is taken to be an impression of a building that does not yet exist at the time of the drawing's preparation; it is made in advance of the executed structure. The illustration reflects the skill of the illustrator in creating a graphic impression when no solid, three-dimensional reality yet exists. As Raymond Meyerscaugh-Walker put it in his book, *The Perspectivist,* "The perspective as the drawing of a project not yet built is one of the few possibilities left to the three-dimensional painter with which the camera cannot possibly compete."

The essence of a design concept is conveyed through a simple and most direct means of graphic rendition of a form/space concept (Fig. 1). Effective drawings depend on an accurate line drawing that delineates an appropriate amount of detail, presents the information from an advantageous viewpoint, and lends a sense of interest to the subject matter (Figs. 2 and 3). From this point on, drawing and sketching become further embellishment beyond the formation of the design and illustration concept (Fig. 4).

Developing the ability to sketch with an economy of line, tone, color, and texture means being able to previsualize, or to train the eye to select the appropriate line weights, values, and colors for the construction of a visual environment. Gathering this information from observing a subject involves processes of visual communication, the goal of which is to quickly grasp the portions of a subject that should be recognizable, familiar, or in need of exaggeration to evoke a desired emotional response.

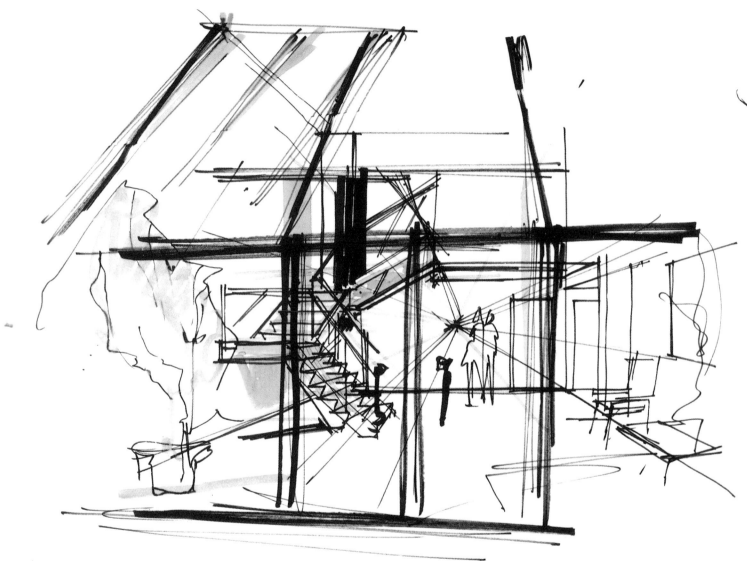

1. A perspective study of abstract space relationships for a building lobby.

2. The visual information added to the initial sketch includes value, texture, and form.

3. A greater organization of information from notes found in previous studies in the rendition of a few values.

4. A refined architectural marker sketch.

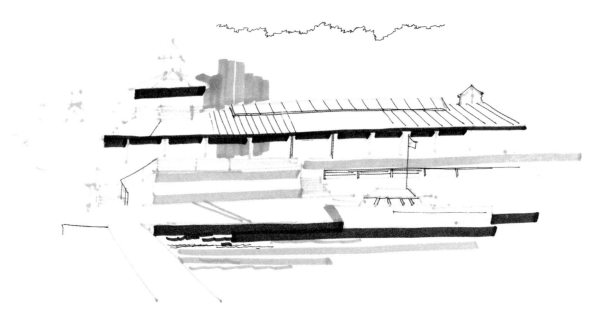

5. A marina, expressed as a simple statement of form through line, value, and texture.

Selective Vision

The ability to make accurate and effective freehand perspective drawings builds confidence and efficiency useful to many preliminary stages of the design process. One of the most important secrets of capturing a scene is learning to achieve the maximum amount of effect through the minimum amount of detail (Figs. 5 and 6). Simplification of details is essential at the outset—what appears complicated in reality has basic, underlying patterns of shape, form, color, and texture that individually or together may form a simple visual pattern and establish the theme for a single sketch or series of investigations (Fig. 7). Selecting various angles of view for a series of brief works exercises the ability to handle perspectives while training the eye to isolate concentrated design elements from a busy environment (Figs. 8 through 10).

6. James Abernethy College for Creative and Performing Arts, expressed through a minimum of line and tonal value.

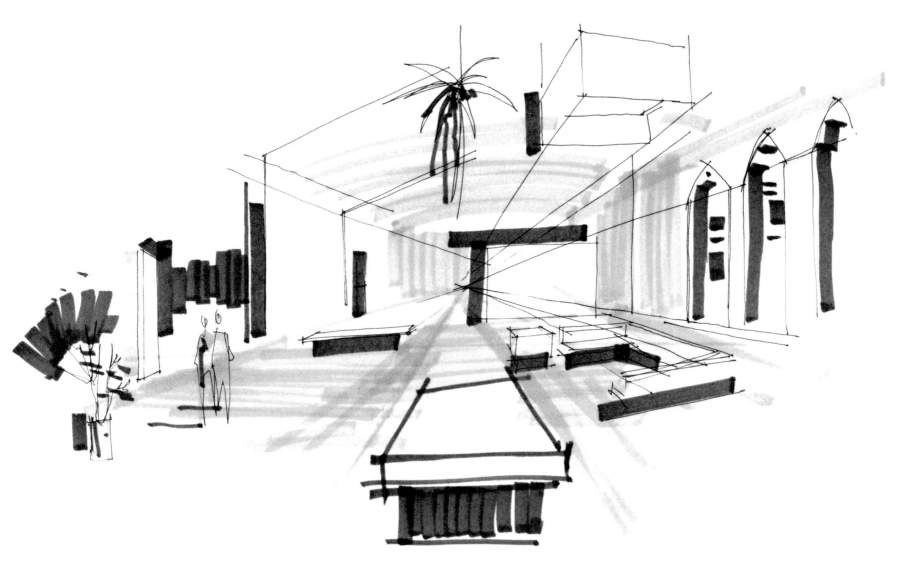

7. The Information Center for James Abernethy College, in dark and light tones.

8 through 10. Three views of the Engineering Building addition at Lawrence Technological University: Figure 8 is an eye-level view closest to the entrance, while Figures 9 and 10 portray the right side of the entrance. The building is given greater contrast in dark, while background buildings fade in the distance in light grays.

9.

10.

11. A value scale in a range of seven gray markers.

Value Sketch

A clear sketch is distinguished by one essential visual element: the value concept. This is a plan for the interpretation of an abstract pattern of light and form and the establishment of an illustration's overall mood. Marker pens aid in this process by enabling the designer to have an efficient and

simple means of establishing the light source and setting the relation of form and space in an environment. The design concept conveyed through a minimum of three values is the basic structure and framework on which the assembled subject matter (composition, value, color, and texture) is suspended, all working to maintain the shape of the original plan of the illustration (Fig. 11). The sketch quickly establishes a visual plan and is usually followed by the development of the subject matter within an environmental setting (Figs. 12 through 15).

The first and most basic pattern, light-middle-dark gray values, should represent approximately 10 percent of the visual information present in the normal tone range of a typical black-and-white photograph (Figs. 16A through 16C). This attitude of an *economy of means* still prevails in sketching, with up to ten available marker values as the designer's interest subtly widens to record a slightly larger reaction of light and form in the subject.

Selecting a marker value or color implies a correspondence between what is observed and what is established in a pictorial space. A dominant, high-key color concept requires a structure of value relationships that represents the lightest range of a value scale; a low-key concept (one having low or dark values throughout) maintains a dark appearance as details are added. The choice of a full range, relative to a quality of light, establishes a concept of atmosphere and color, which in turn should be followed consistently in a study sketch or more elaborate drawing (Figs. 17 through 20).

Effective marker drawings are also considered to be somewhat *impressionistic.* They can express a quality of light that lends visual interest and excitement. The effects of dappled, striking, reflective, intense, or luminescent light establishes surface patterns of interest, in addition to the illumination of objects and environments (Figs. 21A through 21C).

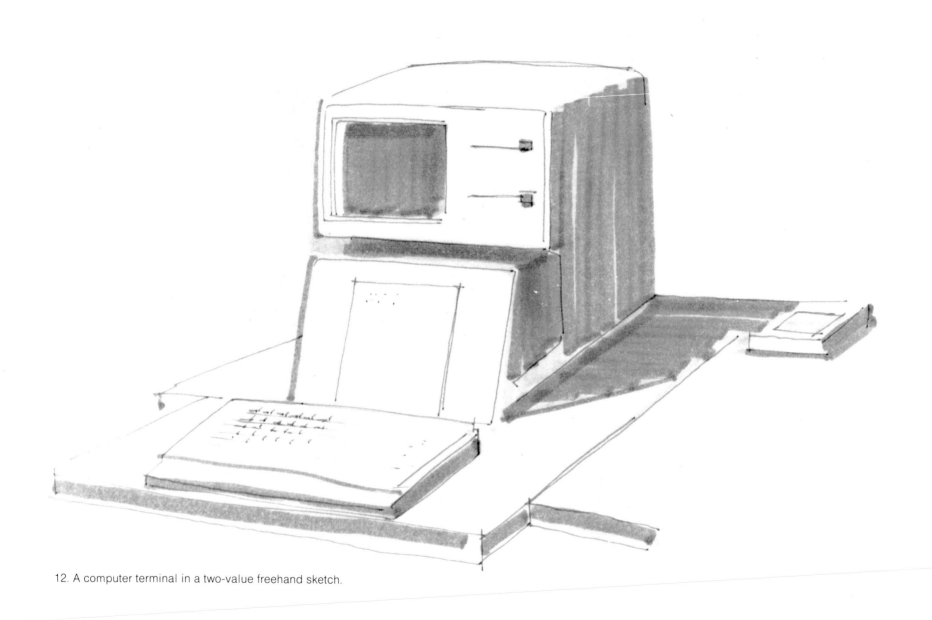

12. A computer terminal in a two-value freehand sketch.

13. A computer terminal in a three-value freehand sketch.

14. A computer terminal in a six-value freehand sketch.

15. A computer terminal in a six-value refinement from earlier studies.

16A through 16C. Studies in a limited value range of Buell Management Building at Lawrence Technological University.

Defining the Concept 19

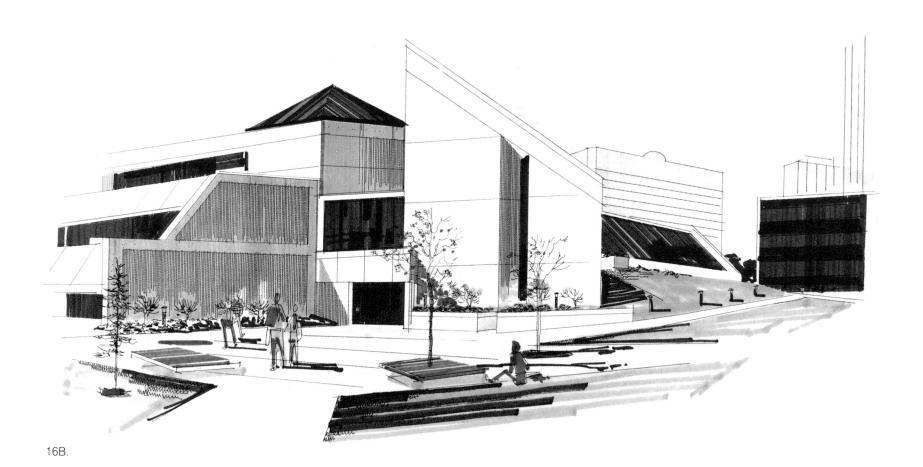

16B.

16C.

17 through 20. Interior sketches of the atrium of Buell Management Building, in a key study of high, middle, and low values and a full value range.

18.

19.

20.

21A. A refined marker sketch reflecting various textures of stone, wood, and concrete and qualities of light reflection.

21B. An interior bedroom study in a range of light to dark values with multiple textures and patterns, with stone, rug, fabric, wall, and tile.

22. Trial study notes for sketch in Figure 23.

Line, Texture, and Tools

There are a multitude of possibilities for achieving texture with markers, and a few basic means or approaches to blending. The objective here is merely to point out the essentials, in order to communicate a basic range of graphic effects, which are further elaborated on in the sketches and illustrations throughout this book.

In the following exercises, experimentation with *mark making,* or the special handling of a marker pen, leads to an increased facility for replicating textural effects found in natural or man-made subjects. Listed below are the appropriate markers and papers to begin creating these effects. Included is a demonstration of a variety of strokes with various tips, the laying in of flat tones over large areas, and several pen-handling methods.

Fine and chisel-tip markers produce a variety of fine and thick strokes, such as those illustrated in Figures 22 and 23.

23. A three-value interpretation of an original pencil drawing by Theodore Kautzky.

24. Trial study notes for sketch in Figure 25.

The difference in line weight or boldness in Figure 23 is merely a function of using different portions of the marker tip. Stroke speed can also contribute to line width, especially on absorbant surfaces, such as sketch papers—a slow stroke allows more ink to flow outward from the marker tip. The middle examples of strokes in Figures 24 and 25 are straightforward products of a chisel-tip marker. These figures also reflect a somewhat wider line, achieved with one of the broad-tip markers. A range of stroke widths is possible, depending on the pen's slant and orientation to the drawing surface. Experimentation with the corners of the chisel-tip pen offers other possibilities, such as twisting or rotating the marker or changing the angle of the pen while stroking or dabbing.

25. A three-value interpretation of an original pencil drawing by Theodore Kautzky

26A and 26B. Trial sketch studies for a lobby interior, expressing simplicity of line, texture, and form.

26B.

As an example, in a three-value (range) study, the absorption of inks into various paper and board surfaces can increase the effects of a value range produced through an overlay of marker strokes. Water-base markers bleed less than oil- or alcohol-base pens on most drawing surfaces. Watercolor pens are appropriate for watercolor paper, quality illustration board, or heavy bond papers. Oil- and alcohol-base pens are more suited for mylar, illustration board, and a wide variety of papers.

A basic list of tools and materials for marker sketching should include: chisel-tip and fine-tip black markers; a technical pen; a light-to-dark range of gray-value chisel-tip markers; bond paper designed for marker use; and parchment tracing paper.

The following examples of sketch studies on illustration board (Figs. 26 and 27) amplify the effects of line and texture, and reflect a light-to-dark progression. These studies are useful rehearsals for analysis of tonal arrangements, structure of elements into a composition, or line, texture, and color qualities.

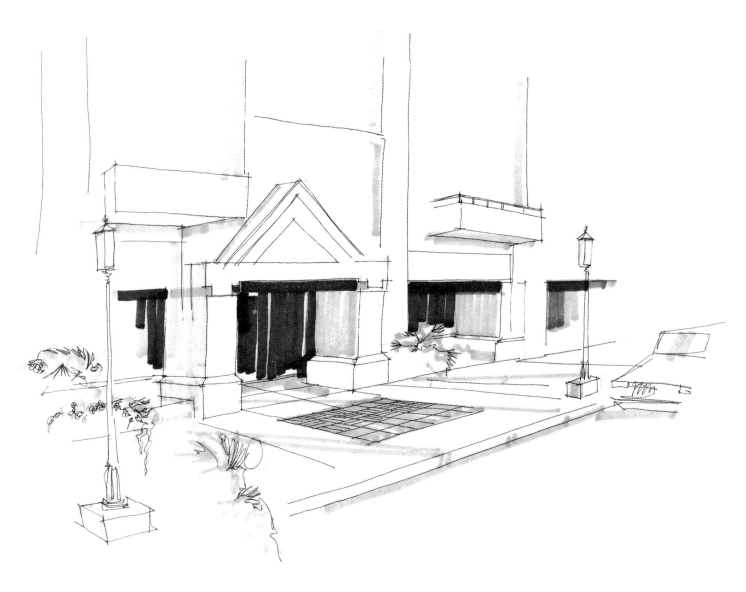

27. A design study of a possible solution to a hotel entrance, in a minimum of line, tone, and simple texture.

28A. This perspective study of a transportation terminal is a spatial analysis in line and tone, and informs the making of the refined drawing in Figure 28B.

28B. A refined perspective sketch of the transportation terminal shown in Figure 28A.

Composition

The idea of creating a picture, whether a painting, photograph, or illustration, begins with the arrangement of form in space and the designer's visual sense. In many circumstances, the center of interest in architectural illustration and rendering is a building, a group of buildings, or an interior view. How the designer assesses the problem of making the building important but not overwhelming is an artistic question with several different types of potential aesthetic solutions, depending on the subject at hand.

Proportion—the relation of the whole composition to the size of the paper on which it is drawn, as well as the relation of the subject and its size to other objects in the picture—is of main interest. The building should not be lost in the surroundings and, conversely, the arrangement of secondary forms around the building should set the stage and lend a counterpoint of secondary interest to the subject. These forms should complement and support the building through the repetition and variation of shape, form, gradation of value and color, and the change in appearance of illumination (Figs. 28A and 28B).

The designer is also clearly interested in achieving a form of balance across the composition. Predominantly dark values grouped to one side of a drawing should be generally avoided in favor of establishing a theme or visual dialogue of value relationships throughout the whole pictorial composition. The use of several line qualities, from delicate to coarse, can also create a hierarchy of visual interest and help orchestrate the picture, giving greatest emphasis to the subject or center of interest. The effective use of blank or white space has as much to do with good composition as does concentrated detail across the entire sheet. Developing one's intuitive sense of the effective role of white space is a great advantage when the brevity of stroke and the concise definition of form and space reflect the intention of simplicity in graphic communication and an economy of means, especially in marker sketching (Figs. 29 and 30).

The first studies should illustrate the importance of keeping the principal element—in this case the building—dominant. Placing the horizon line or the subject itself in the center of the composition is to be avoided; it is usually better to locate the horizon line slightly above or below dead center and to move the subject or main interest area to the right or left and above or below the exact page center (Fig. 31). Supporting elements, such as neighboring buildings, should be placed to the right or left of the main subject to allow the subject to be viewed in its natural setting and environmental context. Whether using a bird's-eye view of a building or a relatively normal eye-level height above or below the subject, it is important that the viewpoint in any drawing be natural, credible, and practical.

A long, low building, as shown in Figure 32 and similar to those depicted in Parts Two and Three, obviously should be rendered parallel to the length of the paper. In the case where a long, low structure runs horizontally, a tree can help frame the composition on one side and more subtle natural elements can do the same on the opposite side. The design principles of unity and balance are just as important and just as applicable in illustration: Equilibrium results when each element of an illustration, including the main subject area, retains its own identity and supports the whole composition. If too many contrasts exist within the subject or in its design and style of illustration, the composition will be unbalanced and will lack unity.

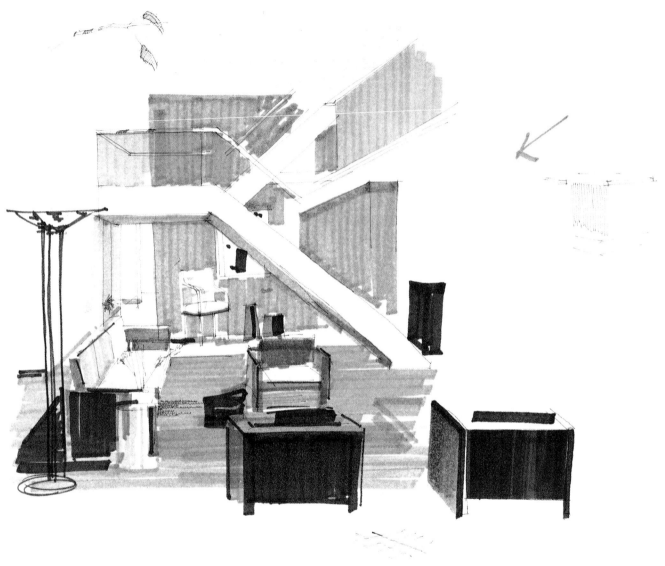

29. Simplicity of line and tone create a planar composition.

30. Refinement with addition of details, based upon the initial study in values in Figure 29.

31. A sketch study with the horizon line moved slightly below the center of drawing

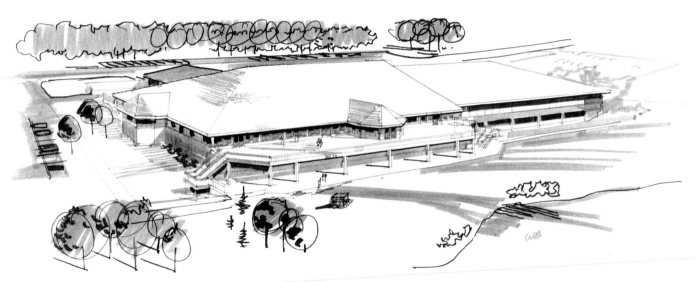

32. A long, low building design is moved slightly to the right of the center of the composition; trees balance the illustration and create interest.

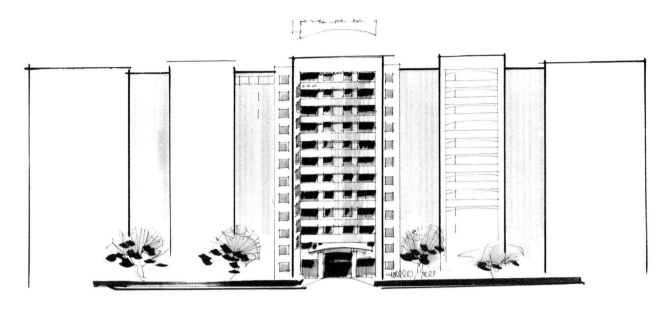

33A through 33C. The economic range of gray values across the relief design of the apartment building reflect a quality of three-dimensional depth through the interplay of shadow and reflection.

Intermediate and Secondary Sketches

The intermediate drawings in Figures 33A through 33C are variations in a design study for an apartment development and demonstrate the gray value range. As elements are developed and conveyed with greater graphic clarity and confidence, they evolve into intermediate or final drawings of greater visual exploration and structure (Figs. 34 through 38). Initial decisions about the mood of an illustration are reflected in the level of illumination, depicted through strong to subtle contrasts in value and the overall role of a high (light values), middle (medium values), or low (dark key values) scheme being dominant in the composition. Because the concept sketch represents the structure upon which an intermediate or final illustration will be built, the flavor of the initial sketch should be maintained throughout the development of detail into more involved drawings. Intermediate and final drawings build an elaboration of subject and detail inherent in the study sketch while making subtle adjustments to value or color, interpreting each successive sketch idea in its own character and significant form. The guiding force behind the development of a design concept is the visualization of an inherently simple image, built from basic relationships of light and form, to give the impression of essential elements.

33B.

33C.

34 through 38. Gallery: Variations of commercial design concepts expressed in a long, low illustration format suitable to the design of the architecture.

35.

36.

37.

38.

39 through 40B. Commercial and industrial developments expressed in a controlled application of light and dark contrasts, with effective use of white spaces: Figure 40A is drawn in chisel stroke, while 40B is a fine-line composition.

Finished and Detailed Marker Sketching

The selection of a full value range relative to a quality of light or color, and its full development within the drawing process, characterizes a development of detail that approaches photographic realism. The following more elaborate drawings are detailed using a fine-line marker and overlays of gray value markers (Figs. 39 and 40). Although markers can achieve a fully realistic and highly detailed effect, as demonstrated in color in later chapters and in the portfolio section of this book, the principal focus of this study is to deal with the ways the creative illustrator and designer grapples with personal expectations, as well as those of the client,

shaping and altering pictorial reality by the way he or she approaches a subject. As these methods are chosen, the sketch and more fully detailed drawings become interpretive rather than merely informative. The freedom to experiment with new and creative means of expression is natural to the processes of making a study sketch, and does not alter the task to portray all elements—color, value, texture, form, and space—in ways that show an awareness of familiar observation, rather than a depiction of disconnected elements merely to achieve a false sense of drama.

40A.

40B.

Tuning in the Color

The colors of marker pens behave much like the transparent washes of watercolor paints. Applying color depends on a good understanding of the *value factor* of a marker color, an overall awareness of what happens when colors are layered or blended over other colors, and an understanding of stroke consistency. It is important to experiment with markers to discover the unlimited potential and combinations possible from a set of one hundred or more original colors.

Some manufacturers are providing refillable units with separate dyes that can be creatively combined. Loading the pen with the original hue mixed from bottled colors allows the freedom to mix individual colors, similar in character to the mixing achieved with an artist's palette or with Flomaster Pens (the original refillable marker pen popular in the 1950s and 1960s).

Beginning with a limited number of pastel colors and light gray values, the designer builds overlays of shade ranges

gradually, while controlling the illusions of color and light in the subject (Fig. 41). The first colors placed over an established black, white, and gray marker sketch reflect the local color, or a subject's surface color appearance, similar to tuning in the color on a television set. In this sense, hues in marker sketching are used to enliven surfaces, portray reflected illumination, and realize textures. Transparent marker hues drawn over gray marker values provide many lessons in understanding how combinations of value and color build toward darker effects when marker colors are layered over and over in a drawing (Figs. 42 and 43). Learning to predict their combined strength in intensity and value is best achieved through direct experimentation with sketch studies and the immediate effects produced from layering of gray values, color over grays, and color over color. Marker drawing pads are an ideal surface for those first study sketches and have the added benefit of allowing one to remove pages from the pad and slide them under a new sheet to "edit" or refine a study in color, value, and texture.

41. A value scale with marker color overlays is a useful tool for anticipating the results of mixing and qualities of hue and light.

42. Automobile and figure silhouettes in gray values.

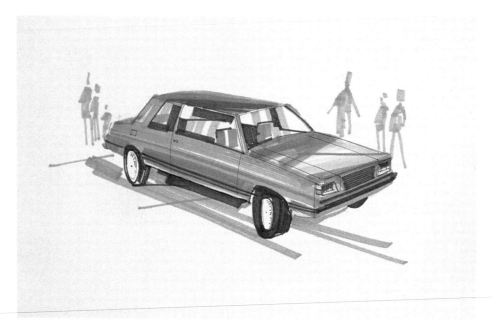

43. Gray values with blue overlays used to tune in the color.

44. A sketch of a railroad terminal at Greenfield Village, Mich., in sepia marker.

Color Silhouette

The pure color sketch often begins with a color silhouette, which establishes the color identity in the subject (or its major elements) and simultaneously presents the hues in a light value that can be increased by value or intensity through successive overlays of color strokes. The simplification of a color scheme for preliminary studies allows the designer an opportunity to test color relationships methodically in successive sketch studies. Beginning with a dark-value hue, such as sepia in Figures 44 through 46, the palette gradually is widened in successive studies, using a sepia-base marker in each drawing, and introducing cool tertiaries, grays, and a wider palette of brighter hues in later studies. Overlay tests performed on tracing paper to explore color variations for one scheme can also be useful when developing intermediate or final drawings requiring great detail and time for execution; however, for brief preliminary sketch studies, seeing a color relationship in a quick, deliberate application is an indispensable aspect of the marker tool and marker drawing process.

45. The machine shop at Greenfield Village, Mich., with sepia and light gray markers.

46. The Souvenir Shop at Greenfield Village, Mich., with sepia, grays, and olive markers.

47. A monochromatic study of a rural setting in sepia marker.

Hue Schemes

Through experimentation with marker hues, the designer usually arranges a hue scheme (including a value range) by limiting color markers to a few hues and values, keeping in mind that many combinations of these hues are possible through stroke repetition, mingling, and distribution. Many mixtures or color moods are possible from only a few colors. Controlling the level of value contrast and hue dominance also contributes to establishing a mood for an environment, as does the planning of illumination, texture, form, and space. Narrowing the possibilities for color climate for a composition from an already-established selection of a few marker colors still requires selective experimentation with their variant combinations, in order to find which of these possibilities best expresses the most appropriate and specific color relationship for the environment and the designer's intent. In Figures 47 and 48, color compositions have been built by giving emphasis to hue, value, or chroma through a description of form and space, and by successive overlays of marker colors. Important highlight areas of a subject are saved as whites or light-value colors, to convey the idea of reflected light or a source of illumination. Limiting the amount of overlay strokes and the number of colors to be used in a drawing is important to the success and impact of a design concept: Too much color will eventually become muddy and lose a sense of color purpose or dominant hue and value character; too little color will leave the viewer with an incomplete sense of the reactions of light on form and a lack

48. A warm gray marker study of Figure 47 with color overlays. Red brings out the color of aged barn wood, once painted red. Shadows in darker hues and values reflect the tie-in between color in the sky (violet-blue) and colors in the barn (red-violet-brown).

49. Studies of an entrance in various groupings of a five-color palette.

of purposeful structure to the arrangement of form and space in the composition. Again, the principles of design fundamentals have always applied to a successful drawing and continue to play an important role in guiding the development and artistic outcome of a sketch composition or final detailed drawing. (*Color Structure and Design* by Richard Ellinger has many clear examples and applications of color strategies for structuring compositions—a very worthwhile and universal language for every serious professional designer.)

Color Climate or Mood

Once you have created a sketch or compositional scheme, examine the possible moods that seem to be suggested by the subject and its shapes and forms. Beginning experiments with rough, loose color studies of basic color groupings, such as a set of complementary colors or a color triad, will stir a response toward further experimentation. Although color selection has a subjective dimension, the study of how a group of colors in various arrangements helps to establish and communicate a mood or emotion most appropriate to the subject requires creativity with a chosen palette (Fig. 49).

Josef Albers, in his instructive and well-known publication *The Interaction of Color,* has carefully discussed how the continuous reinterpretation and elaboration of a select group of colors result in the creation of a display of variant color-grouping possibilities. This in turn gives the designer and artist an opportunity to visualize the most appropriate color combinations for a given form and application.

Making the color statement support the vitality of a well-executed sketch and further the goal of defining the subject in its appropriate climate often requires many revisions and trial sketches. Subtle adjustments of hue, value, and chroma and thorough experimentation with a selected palette of colors lead to greater refinement, fine-tuning the color composition.

50. A sketch of an office building with gray marker base. The dominant building color is brown, while subordinates are blue and green.

Compositional Schemes in Color and Light

Constructing a hue scheme for a single building or group of buildings and their surrounding environment can be approached by establishing a dominance of one hue or hue range with subordinate hues, and applying strong or subtle value contrasts to a composition (Figs. 50 and 51). The examples in Figures 52 through 56 call attention to various schemes that make the color study sketch effective.

Predominant in these works is the underlying principle of a careful value plan in black and white and a conscious selection of color relative to its qualities of light and dark. Once the foundation of careful composition is constructed in line and tone for a subject, it is then possible to provide interest through color overlays or improvisation with color detail and nuance.

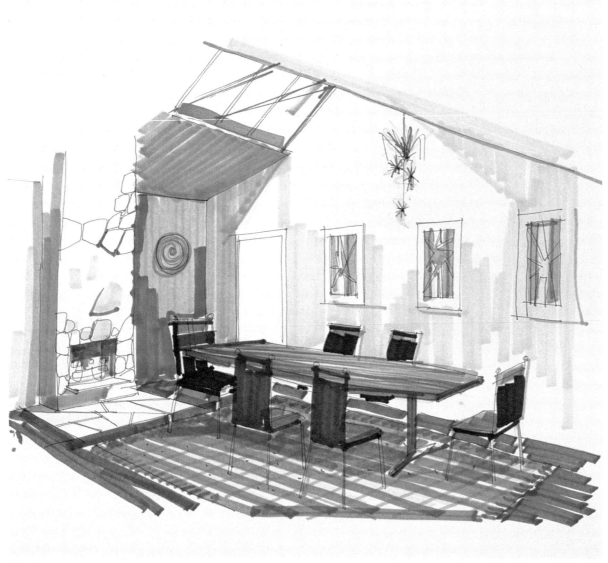

51. A sketch of an interior conference room, largely in gray marker base, using rust marker as a dominant with very subtle blue and green accents.

52 and 53. Two watercolor interpretations from an original watercolor by Theodore Kautzky reflect variations in the execution of color and form.

53.

SKETCH FALLING WATERS
ROY STRICKFADEN

57. Fallingwater, Bear Run, Pa.

STRAITS LINE DOCK—MACKINAW CITY
ROY STRICKFADEN

58. Harbor View, Mackinac Island, Mich.

59. Fishing Village, Kennebunkport, Me.

60. Residential Street, Mackinac Island, Mich.

61. Horse and Carriage, Mackinac Island, Mich.

62. Cable Car, San Francisco, Calif.

63. Roadside Shop, St. Augustine, Fla.

64. Outdoor study in watercolor of a lighthouse, Alpena, Mich.

SITE STUDY JACKSONVILLE BY ROY STRICKFADEN

Part Two:
Establishing Form
and Space

A very quick sketch has much in common with writing. Selecting a marker for drawing should be as simple as selecting a pen for writing. It should be possible to capture the essentials of a busy subject quickly, whether one is working directly from observation, memory, or photographs, just as easily and as freely as words are jotted down as a reminder of something. Stroke simplicity establishes a graphic character through the use of curved, straight, or jagged lines, which should be maintained instinctively throughout the sketch study. The suggestion of detail should also be kept to a minimum in order to avoid overemphasizing subordinate elements. Similarly, the role of contrast, in value and in hue, can help to stimulate interest and provide a focal point for the sketch composition. The examples of building exteriors, interiors, and cityscapes on the following pages underscore various composition elements that make the study sketch effective. Providing interest, defining form and space, and animating surface texture all are aspects of the design environment that are important to both illustrator and client.

65. Many compositions of exterior views, such as this residential proposal of buildings, begin with a simple line sketch that positions the subject relative to the pictorial elements of foreground, middleground, and background space. The value range is then developed within the sketch, which attempts to organize or link the patterns of light, shade, and shadow into a unified and cohesive design instead of allowing them to become scattered throughout the illustration. The addition of vital elements of entourage are included in the composition and sometimes borrowed from areas adjacent to the subject, to enhance the interest of the illustration.

Although the goal in architectural sketching is an economy of elements and simplicity in execution, this does not mean the process will be smooth and effortless, or that the finished sketch will look that way. Finished designs and illustrations do not necessarily look like the original schemes and doodles. The final drawing is fluid; the process is given to fits and starts. The illustration reflects poise and technical confidence; the process entails fussing and moments of indecision.

The organization of detail in a composition is primarily the result of note-taking (Fig. 65). From the earliest days of an active professional's involvement in design and illustration, a passion for taking notes becomes as natural as the instincts to look, to think, to feel, to recognize, to remember (Fig. 66). The

66. This composition of visual notes for an office complex is more dynamic if the center of interest is moved laterally to create a more interesting division of space. The composition of a sketch should be in equilibrium or balance with the overall distribution of weights or values and shapes throughout the picture. More interesting compositions can be derived from experimentation with various proportions of black, white, and middle tone values, as well as from proportional use of color.

note is evidence of the drive for accuracy. It is also a safe harbor where detail, with its bits of intelligence, can slip into a protected room for later investigation, translation, and deciphering.

Sometimes the notes for a drawing are the only drawing (Fig. 67). Dedication to a fragment, which is not itself a drawing, provides an illustrator with the driving desire to spend all that time with what might seem to others to be non-existent or, at the outset, lifeless.

Everyone has a memory with precious odds and ends roaming around. We recognize in ourselves a capacity for viewing life's procession as a collection of shards. It makes sense, therefore, that original and creative illustrations, for all their apparent seamlessness, should be formed of brief notes and discarded bits (Figs. 68 and 69). This sense of being *guided* by imagination—rather than being its master—is a trademark of an authentic experience of creativity.

67. Study notes of trees.

68 and 69. Both of these studies in perspective for an illustration of a summer resort make negative areas work as an abstract pattern.

69.

Le Corbusier kept seventy-three notebooks, amounting to over four thousand pages, documenting the entire life of a great architect. He often referred to this companion as his "sketchbook," and remarked, "Don't take photographs, draw; photography interferes with seeing, drawing etches into the mind." The words of Eugene Delacroix also communicate a note of purpose: "You should always carry a sketchbook with you and become so proficient and absorbed in quickly capturing the very essence of your subject that if a man were to jump from a window within your view, you could capture his expression before he hit the ground."

Sketching Exteriors

The perspective sketch from a well-chosen viewpoint is the standby of many design professionals, and often dozens of quick studies are made in search of the most advantageous view (Fig. 70). Walking around the design subject, vignetting as many conditions as possible, is essential to developing a sense of the architecture and related spaces. The power and excitement of light, through color, reflections, contrasts, and direct shadows, are powerful tools when the hand that delineates the building is connected to the mind that completely conceives it (Fig. 71).

What is important in establishing the concept for form and space is not so much the mechanical accuracy of the perspective as the visual perception of the use of light and portrayal of ambience (Figs. 72 through 75). This is natural for the quick marker drawing, using a single medium or in combination with other media, such as watercolor, pastel, ink, and airbrush. Most designers are too busy to make a mechanical perspective; it is easier to draw a few construction lines and do the rest by experience. This can be done in a fraction of the time it takes to make a mechanical layout.

70. This corner perspective of a commercial shopping center takes advantage of the abstract patterning of important sunlit white shapes.

The activity of sketching in the design process can sometimes last for several weeks—continuously preparing overlays and developing schemes, ideas, and diverse attitudes about form and space in architecture. In a mall environment, the relation of graphics, signs, color, light, and scale can all come under scrutiny in sketch form (Fig. 76). Isometrics, perspectives, and plan sketches are the tools of visualization for developing design concepts.

Quick perspectives are regularly used for in-house design discussions. Many firms do not require the use of renderings; instead, they make use of such tools as study models and quick sketches, which provide maximum work/study benefit for the time spent. Perspective sketches are equally effective as tools for discussions with clients as they are between design professionals (Figs. 77 through 80). Sketches are important communication links between designer and client: In many types of client/designer interactions, sketching provides an informal bridge toward a closer understanding of the interests of both parties. Furthermore, the ability to sketch while holding a conversation is a skill that many professionals find useful—many clients enjoy seeing the creative process actually occur before their eyes and consider this a cooperative initiative on the part of the design professional. This adds to the dimension of communication between client and designer, bringing a special charm and closer bond of participation.

71. A perspective study for a high-rise office building uses flagpoles in the background as a foil for the building.

72. A holiday street scene in vivid hue accents.

73. A study of light and reflection ties buildings together with a seascape.

74. A barn study in marker expresses a strong relation to a flat ground plane.

75. This barn study in watercolor expresses relation of surrounding scale to telephone poles and entourage.

76. A commercial shopping plaza.

77. A sketch of a rural setting.

78. A sketch of a harbor and boats.

79. A sketch of a tanker in harbor.

"ARDGLAS" A FISHINGTOWN IN COUNTY DOWN

80. A sketch of a seaside village.

Sketching Interiors

Recently, interior design drawing has moved away from previous expressive forms to become increasingly concerned with decorative aspects of design—contract and space planning of offices and commercial spaces—and with drafting documents of mechanical production for impersonal spaces. Although the interior designer finds much activity today in commercial work, in many ways interior drawings (along with architectural sketches and drawings) have also become more highly regarded as a collectible form of art and design.

Interior designers and architects use quick study sketches with a subconscious skill derived partly from training, partly from the special properties of the medium, and partly from the natures of perception and cognition (Fig. 81). Although quick sketches are commonly taken for granted in current practice, because they seem so informal, easily made, and easily discarded, the substance of the text shows that sketching is more than just a handy way of working out a design problem. Indeed, the origin, nature, and methods of obtaining knowledge in design can be explained largely in terms of the properties and working processes of the study drawings in which programs are formulated.

81. A sketch of a restaurant interior, emphasizing contrast in value and bright colors.

82A through 82C. Notation sketches.

Quick sketches are usually made to record the bare essentials of an interior scene or imaginative concept (Figs. 82A through 82C). The design stops before getting bogged down in details. With the assistance of mental and written notes, the designer may later begin abstract compositions from mental images of the scene and original vision (Figs. 83A through 83C). The designer then has several more opportunities to return to the scene and compare sketch studies with original inspiration or source material for the design and decide whether to edit or move away from the source through other means and ideas (Figs. 84A through 84F).

82B.

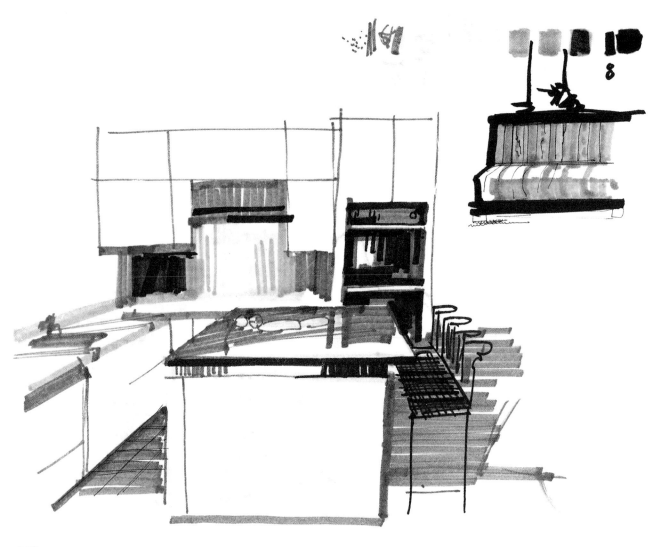

82C.

83A through 83C. Beginning the sketch in line and value for kitchen interiors.

83B.

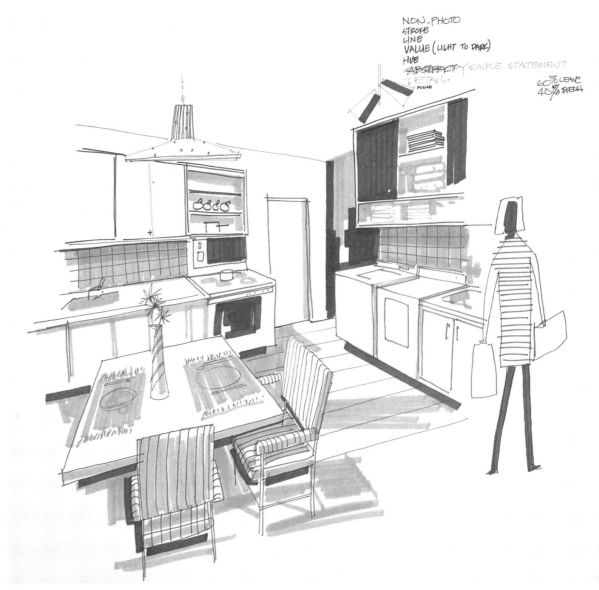

83C.

SIMPLICITY MARKER STROKE

84A through 84F. Although interior arrangements of appliances and color schemes may vary, this series of interior kitchen sketches sufficiently defines each object within the space in order to describe the separate functions within the kitchen environment.

84B.

KITCHEN
PERSPECTIVE STUDY

84C.

84D.

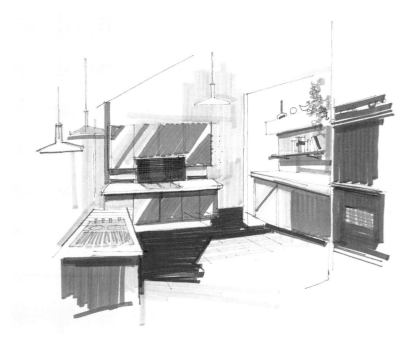

84E.

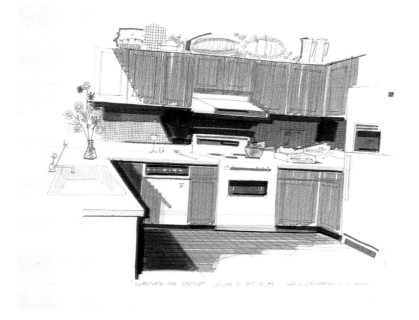

84F.

In the case of small residential and interior projects, the *presentation sketch*—as opposed to a more elaborate and costly presentation rendering—is a very useful device (Figs. 85A and 85B). The term *presentation* perhaps has its roots in advertising and promotional work, where firms made presentations to clients in order to show proposed schemes for new products and images (Fig. 86). The presentation sketch is by nature quick, and is usually produced as part of the design process (Figs. 87A through 87C). These sketches are often better suited for reproduction than a more complex and elaborate drawing. While highly refined renderings lose sharpness and other qualities of fine detail when subjected to the coarse halftone screen used in most printing, the more direct, simple form of a color sketch is likely to better survive printing processes and convey a sense of direct communication from the designer.

85A and 85B. Living rooms expressed in warm hues.

85B.

86. Bright color accents in a neutral scheme for an interior living space.

87A through 87C. Residential interiors.

87B.

87C.

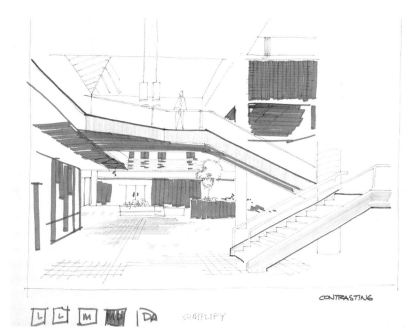

CONTRASTING

SIMPLIFY

88A through 88C. A preliminary sketch sequence of lobby interiors with presentation sketches.

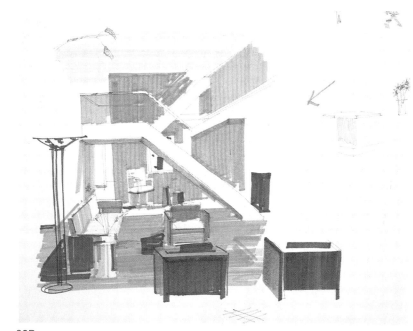

88B.

Sketches made for interior spaces often must anticipate more than one source of illumination. Combinations of natural and man-made light often occur in the same setting. Early black-and-white sketches may use value contrast in a compositional scheme to convey the idea of an illumination quantity present in an environment. Early color studies may add the dimension of illumination quality (or temperature) by establishing a warm or cool temperature scheme. The designer may also choose to further refine aspects of both quantity and quality of light, as well as characteristic reflections, through more careful analysis and experimentation with marker blending of value and hue ranges (Figs. 88A through 88C).

88C.

In many ways, the designer focuses on the ambience of interior spaces through an arrangement of elements: line, value, texture, color, shape, and form (Fig. 89). The ambience of a space is often a direct result of the orchestration of these visual elements, many of which are distilled directly from notes made from observation or from within a space, into an abstract pattern of interest (Figs. 90A and 90B). The attributes of human form, nature, and the many surrounding elements that lend scale and an understanding of a space are also vital. However, the deliberate sketch qualifies and informs many of the decisions yet to come, including the final arrangement of details, by establishing the point of view and a basic, abstract pattern to which everything else will be related (Figs. 91 and 92).

89. A preliminary sketch for an interior living space.

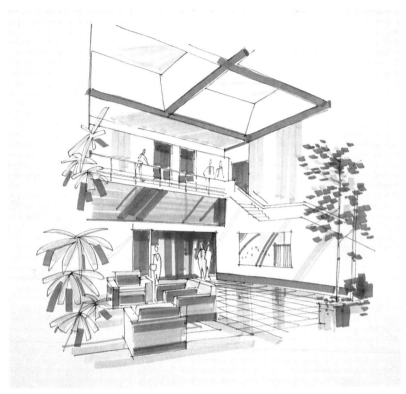

90A and 90B. Intermediate sketch studies of office and lobby environments.

90B.

91.A presentation sketch, in line, of a conference room.

92. A presentation sketch of a mall interior.

FOOD

TARRINGTON

PERSPECTIVE   ROY STRICKFADEN

Cityscapes

The presentation sketch is most often a perspective. The ability to sketch freely in perspective is the result of becoming familiar with two methods of visual communication: drawing from observation (or "by eye") and understanding how to make an accurate mechanical perspective. Producing mechanical perspectives is especially helpful in converting a large concept for a drawing of a city, a complex building form, or aerial studies of urban environments into a correct perspective (Figs. 93 through 96).

For many studies involving complex forms or shapes in great number, it is worthwhile to make a constructed perspective layout as an underlay sheet over which to compose the subject. The controlled mechanical drawing gives the designer an opportunity to sketch more freely, confident that the result will be consistent with the perspective and convincing in its portrayal of the space that it depicts.

Within the scope of professional practice, many design disciplines are constantly making attempts to simplify the presentation process, trying to make presentations more comprehensible to the client even if the process becomes more complicated, and devising methods to help the client to "see" the proposed concept with clearer visual awareness and understanding.

93. A perspective sketch emphasizing a building entrance.

94. A perspective sketch emphasizing a chapel entrance.

95. A sketch of a street entryway in San Miguel de Allende, Mexico.

96. A sketch of a gate entrance from a church and market area in San Miguel de Allende, Mexico.

Quick and effective sketches must be spontaneous—the illustrator must find the most important object to use to establish the mood of the illustration (Figs. 97 through 99). If the subject is complex, the appropriate entourage is arranged with the subject into an effective pattern of form and space and illustrated with marker and, perhaps, related drawing tools (Figs. 100 through 102).

97. A sketch of Mackinac Island, Mich.

98. A sketch of Greenfield Village, Mich.

99. A sketch of a bicycle shop in Greenfield Village, Mich.

100. A sketch of a cityscape in Spain.

In large offices, where work is billed on a cost-plus basis, infinite pains can be exercised to produce exquisite drawings. But today, even large firms seek to simplify the presentation process. In many instances, a presentation that may have taken three months to produce will be viewed by the client only for an hour or so. For these reasons, many offices attempt to show the best viewpoint of the subject, playing down details and producing the most effective mood and setting possible.

Because clients usually enjoy knowing how a project evolved and what alternatives were considered, early sketch studies, diagrams, notes, and any other devices the architect can think of are included in many presentations. Often more than one scheme relating to a single project is also developed for the presentation (Figs. 103 and 104).

Sketching such subjects as urban environments and aerial perspectives also challenges and advances the designer's understanding of the structural nature of mass that underlies all forms, and helps the artist recognize its presence in variously interjoined combinations (Figs. 105 through 108).

101. A sketch of a cityscape in Ireland.

SAN MIGUEL ALLENDE MEXICO BY Roy J Strickfaden

102. A sketch of a cityscape in Mexico.

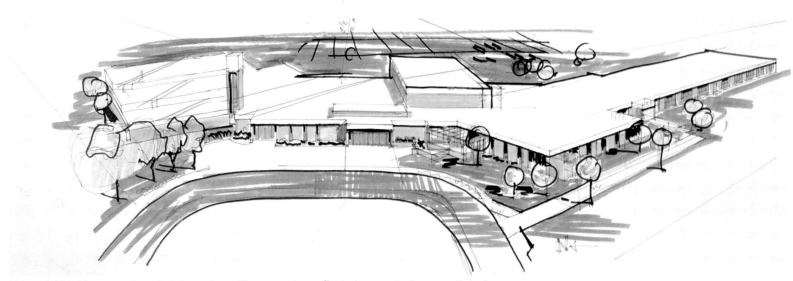

103 and 104. These marker sketches of an office complex reflect changes to the overall design.

104

105. A low aerial marker study of an office building.

106. A low aerial marker study of a business complex with an adjacent office tower.

107. An aerial study for presentation of a condominium and harbor project, in fine-line with marker color.

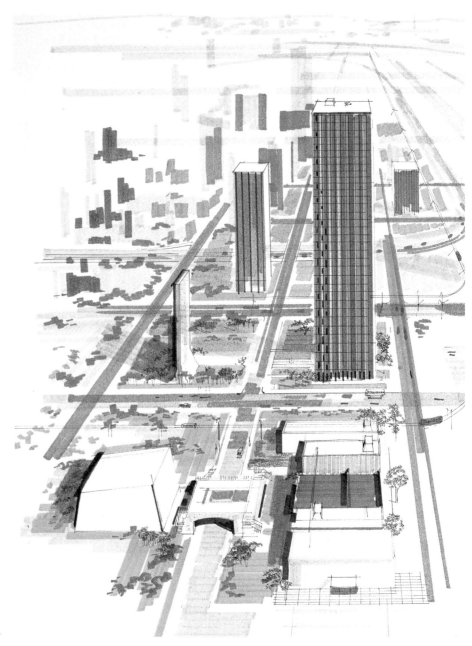

108. A high aerial study for presentation of office tower developments.

Part Three:
Visual References

Architectural Details

The purpose of sketching in the development of details is not always obvious. We tend to think of the sketch as a vehicle for abstract, large-scale ideas and to leave detailing for another phase—most likely during the construction process. Often, however, an interesting detail sketched during the early part of the design process can develop far greater importance later in the design (Figs. 109 and 110).

There are many dimensions of interior architecture that invite interest for sketching, including furniture, major entrances, people, prominent windows, and landscaping, to name a few. Furniture has many possibilities that can be developed into a focal point (Figs. 111 through 113). The number of designs and the ever-expanding selection of material coverings for furnishings provide challenging surfaces, colors, and textural effects (Figs. 114 through 117).

In the design of the contemporary office environment, built-in wall units, conference tables, chairs, and couches can sometimes have greater thematic or focal interest than the project design into which they are placed. Desks, tables, and computers, along with a vast array of accompanying storage units, offer an abundance of technological forms for detailing in sketches of today's workplace (Fig. 118). Figures 119 and 120 illustrate a conference room, a common situation in which the role of surfaces, colors, and textures play an important part in the interior project. Sketch studies of automobiles (Figs. 121 through 123), along with studies of human figures and landscape materials (Figs. 124 through 126), are also important as components in the overall architectural environment.

109. A sketch page of figure silhouettes and other notes.

110. A sketch page of figure silhouettes and landscape plan graphics.

111 through 113. Desk and executive chairs in value studies with color washes.

112.

113.

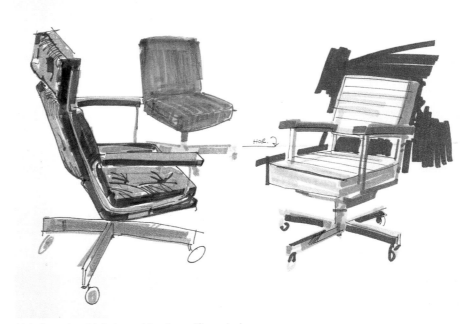

114. A study of fabric and leather office chairs.

115. A study of fabric and chrome office chairs.

LOUNGE CHAIR
DESIGNED BY FRANCK & SAUER
VECTA CONTRACT GRAND PRAIRIE

117.

116 and 117. A study of fabric office chairs.

118. A computer terminal.

119. A preliminary sketch.

120. An intermediate sketch.

121 through 123. Value studies of automobiles with color washes.

122.

123.

124 through 126. Tree studies in gray value marker, marker color, and watercolor.

125.

126.

Marker Variations and Other Media

Toned papers offer some advantages for marker drawing when compared to the commonly used white drawing paper. They have an effect on marker hues that dulls the color's intensity. Because marker hues are quite brilliant, working on toned surfaces can help harmonize the color composition of an illustration (Fig. 127). Toned papers are commonly available in art supply stores but can also be produced through the Diazo reproduction process usually available in a design office. In either circumstance, they offer the advantage of efficiency—if there is insufficient time to apply color to the entire composition, a smaller and perhaps more central portion can be colored (Figs. 128 through 130). This vignette technique is common in the repertoire of many illustrators and allows color to retain its impact without becoming lost in a field of white. By applying color to the center of interest and gradually fading the color and contrast as the drawing expands outward, the artist efficiently allows the drawing to retain a focal point of color and illumination.

Diazo prints are probably the most widely used print media in architecture offices, and can be considered toned papers. A sketch on drawing vellum or mylar may be printed at a faster than normal printing press speed, which results in a toned background. Marker colors can then be applied directly to the print or to other prints made from the original drawing (Figs. 131 and 132).

Common reproduction paper colors are black, blue, and brown. The paper color and its tone can be coordinated for a particular scheme with a compatible range of marker hues. The blue-line print is suited for a cool-hue scheme, and brown-line for a warm-hue scheme. Greater visual contrast can also be created by using a toned paper with a complementary range of marker hues. Gray backgrounds produced from a black-line print are neutral, applicable for most variations of marker hue schemes from warm to cool.

Traditional artists's drawing tools can offer an expanded range of effects in combination with markers, especially for more finished and detailed renderings: technical pens can play an important part in a marker drawing through an expanded range of ink colors for finishing fine details; the traditional ruling pen used with tempera paint or designer's gouache can be effective over marker drawings on print papers for details requiring line control and bright or stark color contrasts (Fig. 133); in many instances, white papers of substantial weight, such as 2- or 3-ply bristol, or illustration boards with a vellum surface, offer a smooth surface and minimal bleeding for marker drawing and improvisation with many related artist's materials. Perhaps the only disadvantage to working on white paperboards is that the original drawing must be drawn directly on the final rendering surface. Graphic aids, such as a light table, lucitograph, and carbon papers, all are helpful to freeing the designer and illustrator to work creatively and imaginatively with graphic images (Fig. 134).

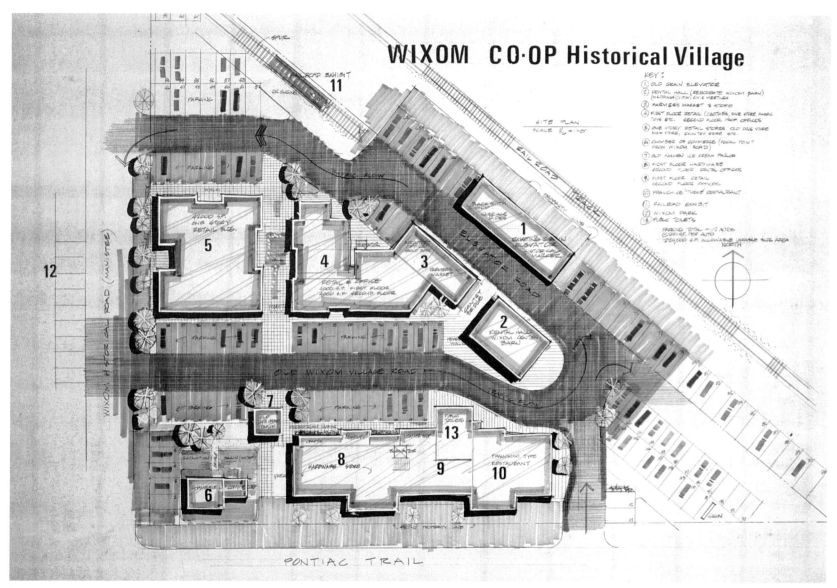

127. A plan graphic for a historical village on light-gray-toned print.

128. A vignette composition in marker on a black-line print, with accents in tempera.

129. A vignette composition in marker on a toned print.

130. A vignette composition on a black-line print.

131. A vignette composition on a toned background.

132. A vignette composition of an apartment building complex, on a light-toned background.

133. A vignette composition of a resort complex, in marker and tempera.

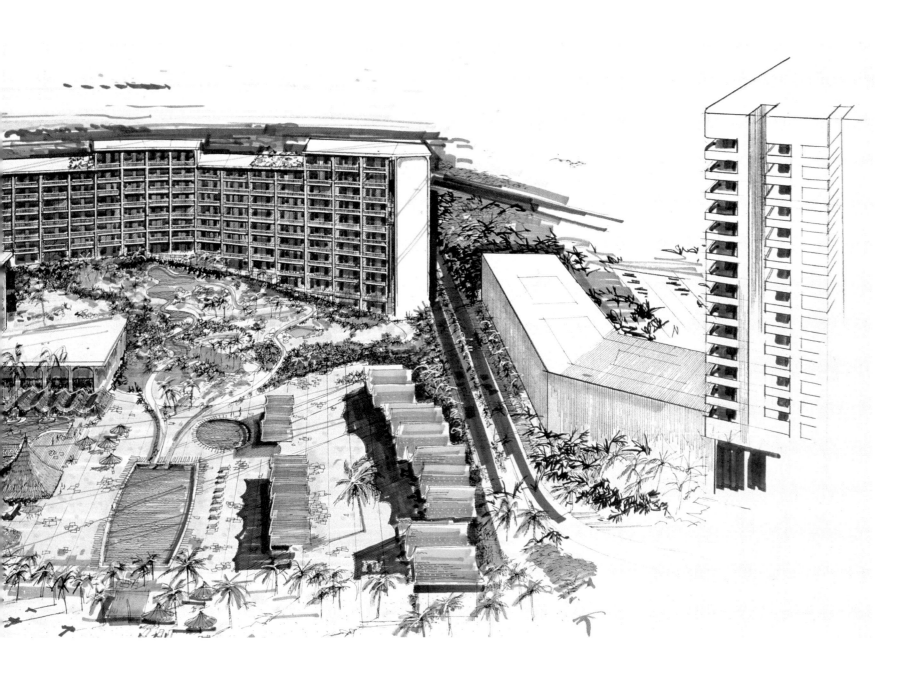

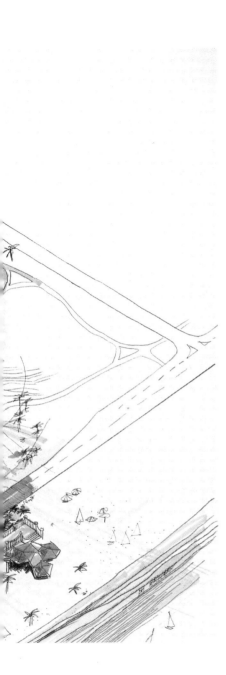

134. A vignette composition of a hotel complex, in marker, tempera, and technical pen.

Travel Sketching

A travel sketch is a special kind of study that enhances the memory and offers an opportunity to record ideas of form and space by emphasizing or omitting details as desired, thereby producing a record with more meaning than the quick snapshot. It implies a personal freedom to choose subject, drawing tools, and the communication mode. It is also an activity with a well-established tradition in art and architecture, and is an important way of having a direct experience with a wide variety of historic and modern buildings, contributing to the understanding of form and powers of analysis.

Artists and architects have always made sketches as brief notes and as a means of laying out general shapes in drawings or on canvas for eventual development into finished art. The tiny sketchbooks of William Turner, housed in the Reading Room of the British Museum in London, are filled with modest drawings in simple strokes of pencil or watercolor from ideas generated during his many trips through England and Europe. Leonardo da Vinci's notebooks, filled with diagrams, computations, notes, and drawings, reflect the creative and analytic dimension of a great scientist and artist. At the beginning of the twentieth century, the sketch held great importance in architectural education at the Ecole des Beaux-Arts: Design students were asked to sketch a design concept in one day and then fully develop this concept in more elaborate drawings and renderings over the next few weeks.

135. A rural study.

The tradition of the quick sketch enabled the instructors at the Beaux-Arts to verify and emphasize originality in the design concept and promote their students's abilities to thoroughly develop one idea. These values in design education helped make the Beaux-Arts reputation, and continue to influence the system of architectural education in modern design training.

The following drawings in this section of Part Three reflect work created primarily in Mexico. Several of these sketches were created directly from observation of public squares and places of interest. A few sketches have been revised and later refined in the studio from brief notes taken on location (Figs. 135 through 147).

136. A historic village.

137. A seascape.

138. A Mexican village.

139. Visual notes of a tavern interior, San Miguel de Allende, Mexico.

140. A revised study of Figure 139.

141. A village street, San Miguel de Allende, Mexico.

VILLA LAURO PEURTO VALLERTA MEXIO WATER MARKERS ROY STRICKFADEN May 1989

142. A beach front, Puerto Vallarta, Mexico.

143. A swimming pool and beach hut, Puerto Vallarta, Mexico.

144. Beach huts, Puerto Vallarta, Mexico.

145. A sundeck, Puerto Vallarta, Mexico.

146. Hacienda, Puerto Vallarta, Mexico.

147. An aerial view of a resort complex, in tempera.

Part Four: Portfolios

Portfolios

Great architectural illustration grows out of the art and skill of balancing illusion with the anticipation of reality, combining the artist's ability to fulfill a viewer's psychic expectations with the delineator's talent to deliver the satisfaction of substance. Because architectural illustrators work between concept and reality, they play the delicate role of exciting our expectations without frustrating our ultimate realizations. Their talent is put to its greatest test, however, when dealing with the exploration of design drawing in the previsualization stage, when they extract ideation from the words and simple sketches of the architect and translate them into clear and useful graphic substance. It is a rare ability, brought to final form as thoughts blossom into beautiful images.

The portfolios that follow, as well as the accompanying descriptive comments from the artists themselves, are the work of a special group of designers. These extraordinary artists deserve appreciation for the ability to draw with exceptional clarity. But even more remarkable is their ability to think, to see, to understand, and to express slight ideas into brilliant images.

KARL H. GREIMEL, F.A.I.A.
Dean, College of Architecture and Design
Lawrence Technological University

William S. Allen

E. R. Baker Associates

John A. Duncan

Ferrero/Maricak, Architects

Carl D. Johnson, F.A.S.L.A.

Richard Rochon

Robert L. Sutton

William S. Allen

William S. Allen, a graduate of the University of Michigan, is a principal in his own practice as a landscape architect and Professor of Architecture at the College of Architecture and Design at Lawrence Technological University. His work in design, illustration, and serigraphy reflects a great sensitivity and enjoyment of drawing. His drawings and prints, in the collections of major corporations throughout the Midwest, show a remarkable awareness of the natural environment, as well as a fluid understanding of the graphic portrayal of the forms of natural materials.

"Throughout my practice as a landscape architect, I have emphasized my role as a designer first and as an illustrator second. In this sense, I use sketching as the primary means to express an idea, a concept, or an intention.

"Although plan-view graphics in landscape design enable a logical design process to evolve, they are not easily understood by a client and sometimes require the use of other views, such as perspectives, elevations, or axonometrics, to better demonstrate the spatial qualities of a design proposal.

"Much of my work is done on blue-line prints. They offer a *base,* or point of preliminary graphic development, which may be further refined to whatever degree of development is appropriate. The use of mylar overlays on a *base* map design also affords great freedom during the design process for graphic treatments and concept development. Markers on mylar can be intermingled into an impressionistic effect, somewhat like the watercolor medium, and they are also easily erased.

"The degree of graphic refinement in my work is dictated by the needs, purposes, and requirements of the project and

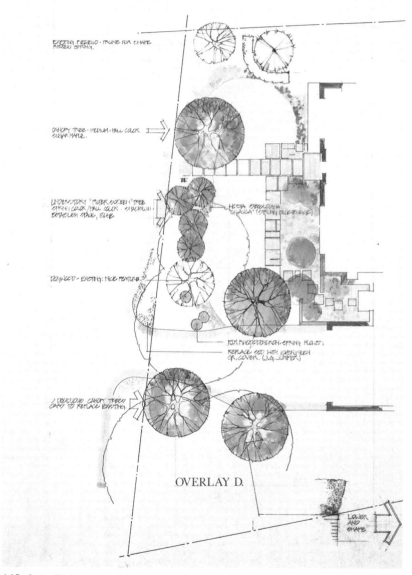

148. A preliminary landscape development for a residential design proposal. The plan includes front entrance development (overlay D).

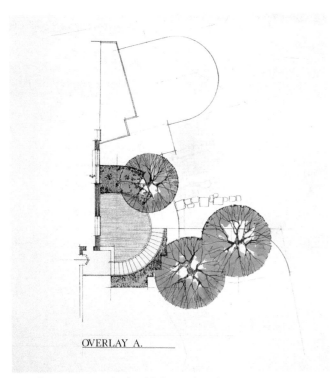

149. Second-story deck with lower-level access
(overlay A).

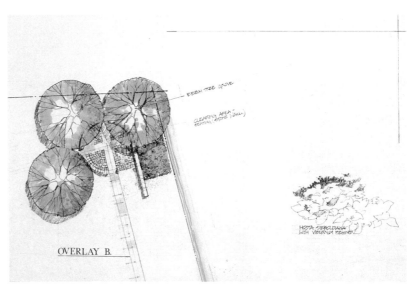

150. Clearing with informal seating wall (overlay B).

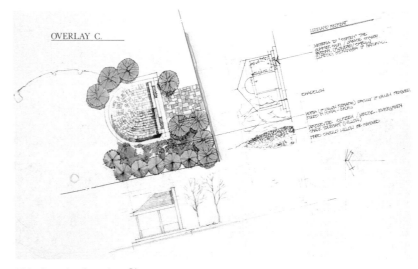

151. Gazebo (overlay C).

client. As my work progresses during the design process, I often continue to refine the qualities of color, form, and detail to approach a greater sense of pictorial realism. In the following samples of a residential design proposal, the client identified four areas of concern. During the design process, the use of mylar overlays provided the flexibility to study alternative schemes for each of the four areas and combine them in the visual field to see their relation as a unified composition. For the preliminary design presentation to the client, all four portions were combined into a single drawing and developed with a greater sense of graphic detail and color development."

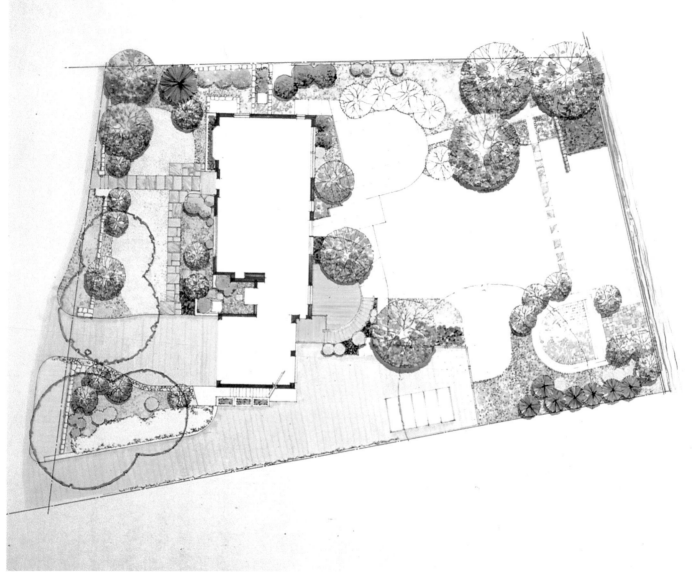

preliminary
landscape
development

scale $\frac{1}{8}" = 1'-0"$

NORTH

WILL ALLEN ASSOCIATES
4305 southshore
pontiac, michigan
48054
313-673-2125
date
revised

152. Composite drawing of overlays A, B, C, and D, constituting the revised plan.

153 and 154. These perspective illustrations were done with marker, airbrush, and colored pencil on cold pressboard. The illustrations were intended to convey to the client the quality of the environment, a sense of place, and the architecture (Finnicum Brownlie Architects).

E. R. Baker Associates

Gene Baker is the founder and principal of E. R. Baker Associates, a multipurpose design firm with far-ranging professional involvements in interior, automotive, and graphic design and illustration. He is a graduate of the Cleveland Institute of Art and has been an instructor of graphic communication at Cranbrook Art Academy. He presently teaches at the College of Architecture and Design at Lawrence Technological University. His admiration for and long friendship with well-known illustrator Syd Mead is reflected in a strong personal commitment to clear communication graphics in his design practice.

"Just like words, perspective sketching in commercial design is a communication technique. Sketches embody both the objectives of transmitting one's concept as well as the means through which the shop's original goal of sales are thoroughly expressed. The immediacy, transparency, and freshness of marker sketching are ultimately vehicles to convey an abundance of design information and professional knowledge. Developing confidence in my abilities of free rendering techniques in perspective drawing has enabled me to cultivate a sense for objects and spaces in the course of my training and professional practice."

155. This interior graphic presentation for a grocery store expresses the scheme of a store within a store.

156. An interior concept for a flower shop, utilizing modular displays.

157. A presentation sketch of an office.

158. A concept for a new front elevation on an existing building.

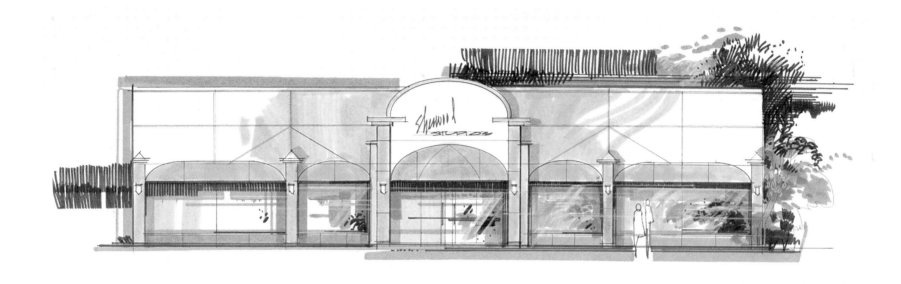

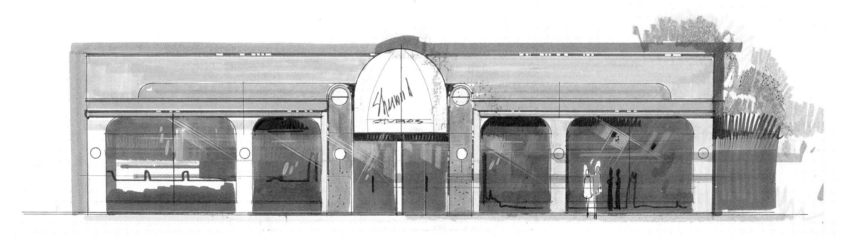

159. A concept for a new front elevation on an existing building.

160. Innovation concept sketch showing awning treatment for a boat club.

John A. Duncan

John A. Duncan is the founder and principal of John A. Duncan Associates, an illustration and graphic communications firm. A graduate of the Art Center College of Design, with a specialization in Industrial Design, Duncan has a rich background, with various projects for NASA, American Motors Corporation, and studies with Eric Curry, a master marker renderer. Duncan's clients include architectural and interior design firms, predominantly in the New York area.

"I have always enjoyed the watercolor medium, from early childhood to my present practice in visual communications. My education at the Art Center concentrated on visual skills— in particular, rendering techniques in watercolor, acrylic, and marker pens. My involvement with interior illustration challenged my abilities to communicate a greater sense of pictorial ambience, rather than defining specific objects. During the process of discovering a new medium, I found many similarities between markers and transparent watercolor. Beginning with light strokes of marker hues and building overlays to a darker or brighter result, the basic theory of adding to the surface was similar to both media. Through experimentation and practice, I have developed confidence with markers, and discovered many combinations with other media, including pastels, colored pencil, and gouache."

161. Proposed hospital renovation (Norman Rosenfield, A.I.A. Architects): marker on brown-line Diazo print.

162. Proposed airport terminal for LaGuardia Airport, New York (William Bodouva Architects): marker and pastel on bond paper.

163. Proposed hotel renovation, New York (Wheel/Gerztoff, Lighting Designers): marker and colored pencil on board.

164. Proposed renovation at Neiman Marcus (Rubano-Mirviss Associates, Inc.): marker on bond paper.

165. Comp for ad shot (Ogilvy & Mather): marker and gouache on bond paper.

166. Comp for ad shot (George Constant, A.S.I.D.): marker and gouache on bond paper.

Ferrero/Maricak, Architects

"Drawing has always been important in our approach to architectural design. Although we employ different drawing techniques in our work, the marker approach is reserved for rapid drawings. A line layout of the general composition without much detail is used as an underlay for the final sketch. A fine-line black marker outline is then traced with more spontaneously added architectural details. Color is then added—broad, light strokes first, followed by more intense color and finely delineated refinements. A sky tone is sometimes sprayed on. Although we use transparent watercolor dyes for this step, spray marker could be substituted with similar results. Architecturally, our work attempts to explore new directions in space and form consistent with our feelings about nature, technology, and the evolving American spirit."

167. A high-speed motor terminal for a city of the future, by Harvey Ferrero.

168. A high-speed motor terminal for a city of the future, by Harvey Ferrero.

169. A study sketch for Annie Oakley Museum, by Harvey Ferrero.

170. A study sketch for Annie Oakley Museum, by Harvey Ferrero.

171. A high-speed motor terminal for a city of the future, by Gretchen Maricak.

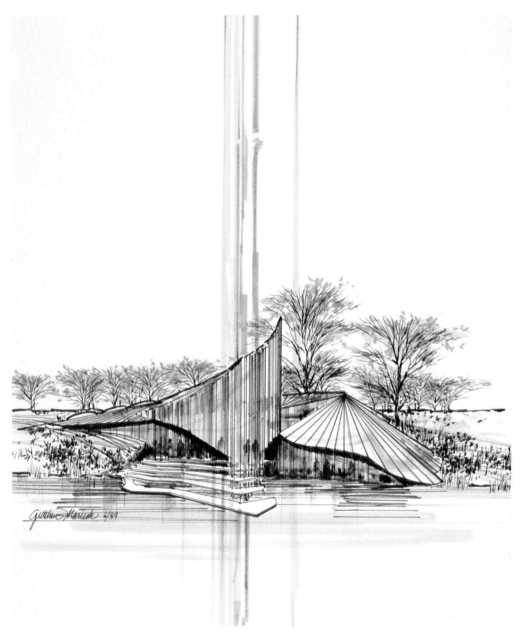

172. A study sketch for a home in the twenty-first century, by Gretchen Maricak.

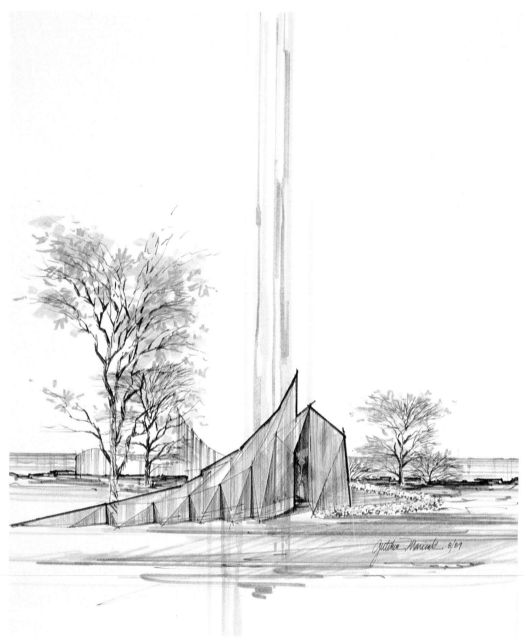

173. A study sketch for a home in the twenty-first
century, by Gretchen Maricak.

Carl D. Johnson, F.A.S.L.A.

Carl D. Johnson is a founding member and principal of Johnson, Johnson & Roy/inc. His work is characterized by a deep understanding of the man-made environment and by his exceptional skill as a designer. He has conducted the basic land-planning courses at The University of Michigan since 1959, and is a Fellow of the American Society of Landscape Architects and visiting professor at numerous universities.

The following thumbnail sketches in marker are representative of a quick, conversational graphic technique that Johnson utilizes to convey the concept of design proposals. Capturing a thought fluidly and quickly, without being encumbered with final rendering techniques, is a necessary tool for communication—a tool that Johnson clearly has mastered, as these sketches amply demonstrate.

174. A conversational sketch prepared during a public workshop for the design of hillside resort condominiums.

KIOSK - SEATWALL
Campus Edge

175. A prismatic color
thumbnail sketch for a
campus kiosk.

176. A schematic sketch of a river's-edge development.

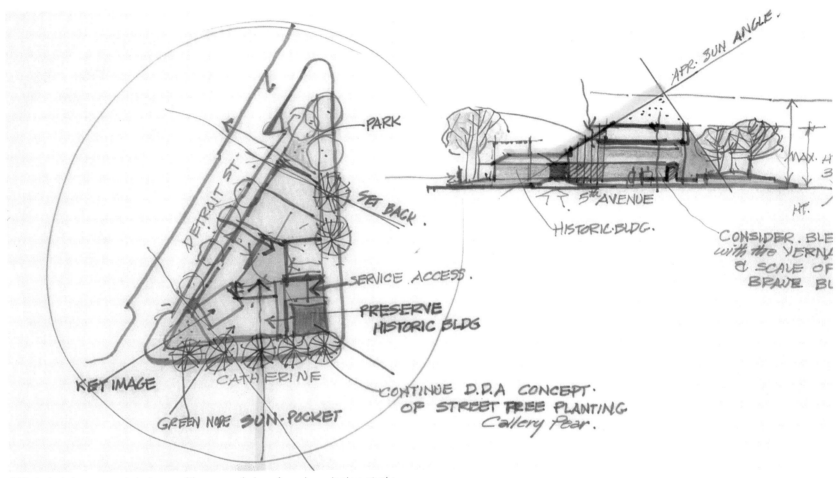

PARK

STA BACK

SERVICE ACCESS.

PRESERVE
HISTORIC BLDG

DETROIT ST.

KEY IMAGE

CATHERINE

GREEN NODE SUN·POCKET

CONTINUE D.D.A CONCEPT·
OF STREET TREE PLANTING
Callery Pear.

APR: SUN ANGLE.

MAX. H
3

5th AVENUE

HISTORIC·BLDG.

HT.

CONSIDER.BLE
with the VERNA
& SCALE OF
BRAVE BL

177. A sketch prepared during a citizens workshop for urban design study.

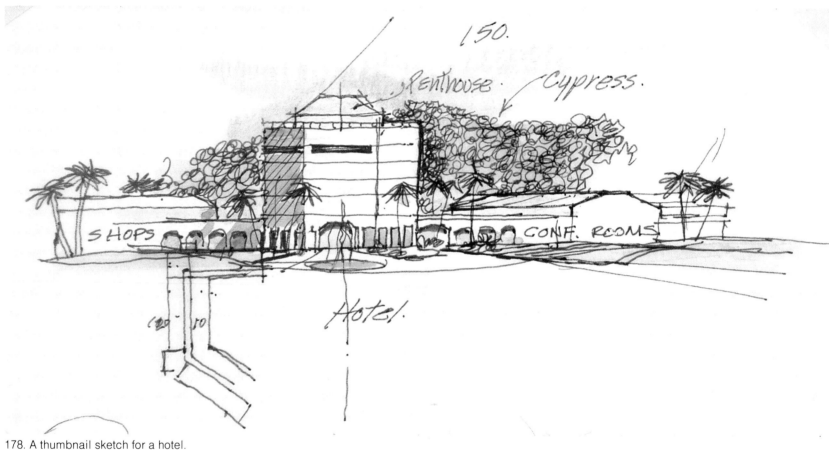

178. A thumbnail sketch for a hotel.

179. A cabin for a teen summer camp.

180. Eli Lilly Conservation study sketch.

181. A watercolor sketch of a Tudor home in England.

Richard Rochon

Richard Rochon, a member of the American Society of Architectural Perspectivists and the New York Society of Renderers, is President of Rochon Associates, Inc., an architectural illustration firm located in Dearborn, Michigan. He has illustrated two books: *Color Model Environments: Color and Light in Three-Dimensional Design,* written by Harold Linton, and his own book, *Color in Architectural Illustration.* He has produced architectural illustrations for many nationally and internationally recognized architectural firms, including Arquitectonica, Cambridge Seven, S.O.M., H.O.K., Ellerbe & Associates, Inc., Smith, Hynchman & Grylls, Inc., Albert Kahn, and many others. In preparation for highly refined color pencil illustrations, he often uses the marker pen to study local color, form, and space in an unrehearsed, freely drawn sketch series.

"Testing ideas in color markers is an ideal way to develop a point of view for an illustration quickly. Markers afford many opportunities to edit or revise and to build images on transparent surfaces, such as tracing vellum, by sketching notes for a space and then sliding the sheets together to see their potential relation. I especially enjoy marker because of its vivid range of hues, which cannot be equaled in color intensity or speed of execution in any other color media. The marker color range also yields excellent results when subjected to electrostatic color reproduction. Marker hues reproduce in much the same character as an original marker sketch and maintain a very similar character of line weight, furthering the creative dimensions of trial compositions and rehearsal studies."

182. Color marker over airbrushed background on electrostatic enlargement.

183. Color marker with airbrushed sky on electrostatic enlargement.

184. Color marker with airbrushed sky on electrostatic enlargement.

185. Color marker on electrostatic enlargement.

186. Sepia and black fine-line marker over gouache on tinted illustration board.

187. Black fine-line marker over gouache on tinted illustration board.

188. Color marker on sepia print of fine-line marker, and pencil drawing on vellum.

Robert L. Sutton

This portfolio sampling of sketches is in commemoration of Robert L. Sutton, whose wonderfully fluid drawings and paintings spanned the realms of commercial art, architectural delineation, and the fine arts. As a graduate of the Cincinnati Art Academy and a member of the American Watercolor Society, he gathered a large clientele of prominent architectural firms throughout the Midwest. His works are in corporate and private collections and have been exhibited in numerous national exhibitions, such as the American Watercolor Society shows in New York City. His commissions have included Borden Corporation, Firestone Corporation, and Columbia Pictures, among many others. The following samples of his work demonstrate his superb control and delightful use of line and form. The elegance and supple manipulation of the vignette composition demonstrated in these sketch studies, and in all of his works, are seldom seen or matched in brief sketches or finished renderings by other contemporary illustrators.

189. A study for a condominium project, in black line marker.

190. A study for a hotel, in black line marker.

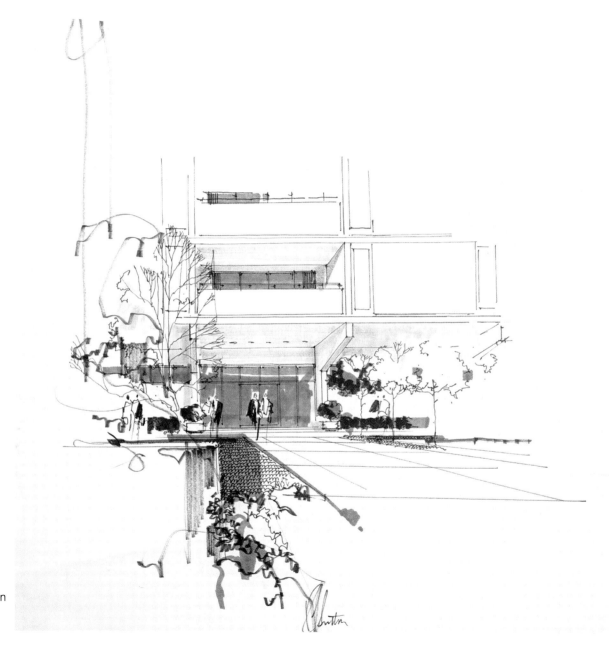

191. A study of a building entrance, in
black fine-line marker with brown
marker tones.

192. A study of a building entrance, in ink with sepia
watercolor wash.

193. A study of public building spaces, in black ink with watercolor washes.

Design Credits

All illustrations are by Roy Strickfaden. Designs as follows:

Figure 32: Fusco Associates, Inc., Southfield, Michigan

Figures 33A through 33C: Mel Sachs, Architect, Farmington Hills, Michigan

Figure 35: Anthony Pucci, Architect, Brighton, Michigan

Figure 36: Mandell Bilovus and Associates, P.C., Franklin, Michigan

Figure 37: Robert Sassak Architect, Ltd., *Focus Hope—Center for Children,* West Bloomfield, Michigan

Figure 38: Young and Young Architects, Inc., Bloomfield Hills, Michigan

Figure 40B: Anthony Pucci, Architect, Brighton, Michigan

Figure 81: Architects: Louis G. Redstone Associates, Inc., Livonia, Michigan

Figure 91: Tiseo and Associates, Inc., Farmington Hills, Michigan

Figure 93: Harley Ellington Pierce Yee Associates, Inc., Southfield, Michigan

Figure 103: John Stewart Associates, Milford, Michigan

Figure 104: John Stewart Associates, Milford, Michigan

Figure 105: Young and Young Architects, Inc., Bloomfield Hills, Michigan

Figure 107: United Design Associates, Cheboygan, Michigan; Farrand Associates, Ann Arbor, Michigan

Figure 129: Harley Ellington Pierce Yee Associates, Inc., Southfield, Michigan

Figure 130: Mel Sachs, Architect, Farmington Hills, Michigan

Figure 131: John Dziurman Associates, Architects & Planners, Rochester Hills, Michigan

Figure 132: Mel Sachs, Architect, Farmington Hills, Michigan

Figure 133: Associated Architects of Aruba, Oranjestad, Aruba; Antonio Muyale and Greg Schiller, Designers

Figure 134: Associated Architects of Aruba, Oranjestad, Aruba; Antonio Muyale and Greg Schiller, Designers

Bibliography

Albers, Josef. *The Interaction of Color.* New Haven: Yale University Press, 1963.

Birren, Faber. *History of Color in Painting.* New York: Van Nostrand Reinhold Company, Inc., 1965.

Bouleau, Charles. *The Painter's Secret Geometry: A Study of Composition in Art.* Harcourt Brace & World Inc., 1980 Reprint of 1963 Edition.

Crowe, Norman and Laseau, Paul. *Visual Notes for Architects and Designers.* New York: Van Nostrand Reinhold, 1984.

Ellinger, Richard G. *Color Structure and Design.* New York: Van Nostrand Reinhold Company, Inc., 1980.

Graham, Donald W. *Composing Pictures: Still and Moving.* New York: Van Nostrand Reinhold Company, Inc., 1970.

Kautzky, Theodore. *Pencil Pictures.* New York: Reinhold Publishing Corporation, 1947.

Kautzky, Theodore. *Ways with Watercolor.* New York: Reinhold Publishing Corporation, 1963.

Kliment, Stephen A. *Creative Communications for a Successful Design Practice.* New York: Whitney Library of Design, 1977.

Linton, Harold. *Color Model Environments: Color and Light in Three-Dimensional Design.* New York: Van Nostrand Reinhold, 1985.

M. I. T. Press. *Le Corbusier Sketchbooks,* Vol. 1., 1914–1948. Cambridge, Mass., 1981.

Myerscaugh-Walker, Raymond. *The Perspectivist.* London: Pitman, 1958.

Rochon, Richard and Linton, Harold. *Color in Architectural Illustration.* New York: Van Nostrand Reinhold, 1989.

Sargeant, Walter. *The Enjoyment and Use of Color.* New York: Dover Publications, Inc., 1982.

Stamp, Gavin. *The Great Perspectivists.* New York: Rizzoli International Publications, Inc., 1982.

Steele, Fritz. *The Sense of Place.* Boston: CBI Publishing Company, 1982.

Wang, Thomas C. *Sketching with Markers.* New York: Van Nostrand Reinhold, 1981.

Index